Beyond the Ivy Vine

Jeaunice Tribue Burnette

Cyberwit.net
HIG 45 Kaushambi Kunj, Kalindipuram
Allahabad - 211011 (U.P.) India
http://www.cyberwit.net
Tel: +(91) 9415091004 +(91) (532) 2552257
E-mail: info@cyberwit.net

Printed at Repro India Limited.

Dedicated

to my mother, Janice Tribue Burnette,

for always believing in me

Acknowledgements

The following poems were featured in literary journals. The poem "mania" was first published in May 2019 in *Stardust Haiku* Issue 29. The poem "children playing" first appeared in *Haikuniverse* on May 26, 2019. The poem "divorce" was first published in the *Taj Mahal Review* in June 2019.

tea roses

spiral with ivy…

jazz in the garden

children playing

in ocean shallows

a pointed fin

mania…
a long abyss
of night

pink and green

colors of sisterhood

forever AKA

cherry blossoms
glide on the river—
a crescent moon

girl scouts

sell cookies on the corner

my throbbing tooth

I run away

through the valley

a murder of crows

whispers

between sweethearts

dinner by candle light

love bugs
joined in passion
an ivy leaf7

our first marriage

counseling session…

rose colored glasses

divorce

her poker face hides

her fears

family reunion

fifty reasons

to be grateful

"only one Barbie"…
little girl falls out
in a tantrum

my cousin sings

to honor our grandma

funeral flowers

a purple heart

for the Vietnam War veteran

I never knew

woman wearing

an orange hijab

my very best friend

auntie's

authentic Indian cuisine—

manna from heaven

counting big rigs

on the highway

long day after work

a lone ant

marches up my shoe

evening at the fair

dripping color

across the sky

a rainbow

bowl of sake

one last serving

under the harvest moon

autumn rain

and maple leaves

a woman struggles with groceries

yoga retreat—

ten sun salutations

to bring in the dawn

my brown skin

the heritage of a proud

and strong race

blues

at the juke joint

moonshine flows

Southern heat

momma combs and washes

my nappy hair

Billie Holiday's

strange fruit…

black bodies dangle

policeman shoots

a twelve year old black boy

black lives matter

"I can't breathe"
one black man's
final words

trees stretch up

towards the constellation

a country village

sunflowers sway

in the wind—

a Tuscan dawn

baby robins chirp

in their nest

drizzling spring rain

lotus

on the pond

cranes ascend

Narcissus

the frog beholds

his own reflection

the fly descends

into the Venus fly trap—

chomp!

gray jay sings in the mist

a blue butterfly

in the meadow

sinking sun

we build

sand castles by the ocean

a beached jellyfish

coral reef

long octopus tentacles

capture a crab

farm children

make snow angels...

the school bell

fumbling

with the flute notes—

a musical recital

a mound of clay

potter is gripped

by creative block

the sound

of barking dogs

I incorporate it into my dreams

boat sails

toward the horizon

too late for farewells

my first gray hair
a million memories
of youth fade

birthday blues arrives

for the Cancer—

her crabby disposition

required

college swim class…

somehow I learn to float

illegal immigrant children

imprisoned in cages

Trump's legacy

insomnia

the midnight infomercials

blurring together

worlds crash inside of me

during the panic attack

heart palpitations

woman with her twenty pearls the ivy vine

the tornado screaming our secrets in the air

Amida Buddha…
light that dispels
the darkness

chanting mantras

with the mala beads

fragrant sandalwood

I offer incense

before Buddha's statue:

Namo Amida Bu

my refuge ceremony

skyping to the UK

technological age of Dharma

I watch the sunset

how many more years

until Pure Land

children nembutsu chanting in the night

girl in contemplation buddha gazing

monk in zazen cherry blossoms falling

stone buddha between me and the dharma

BIO

Jeaunice Tribue Burnette is an aspiring poet. Her work has been published in *Stardust Haiku*, *Haikuniverse*, and *Taj Mahal Review*. She is a member of Alpha Kappa Alpha Sorority, Inc. Ms. Burnette is also a Pureland Buddhist. She graduated from Georgia Southwestern State University with a Bachelor of Science in Psychology. She currently resides in Albany, Georgia, USA.

www.ingramcontent.com/pod-product-compliance
Lightning Source LLC
Chambersburg PA
CBHW051821130726
47987CB00003B/1357